Astro
The Steller Sea Lion

By Jeanne Walker Harvey

Illustrated by Shennen Bersani

Astro is not an ordinary sea lion. He is a Steller sea lion. He lost his mother when he was only a few days old. No one knows what happened to her.

Luckily, a scientist spotted Astro, hungry and all alone, on an island off the California coast. The young pup was brought to The Marine Mammal Center, a place that cares for sick, hurt, and stranded marine mammals.

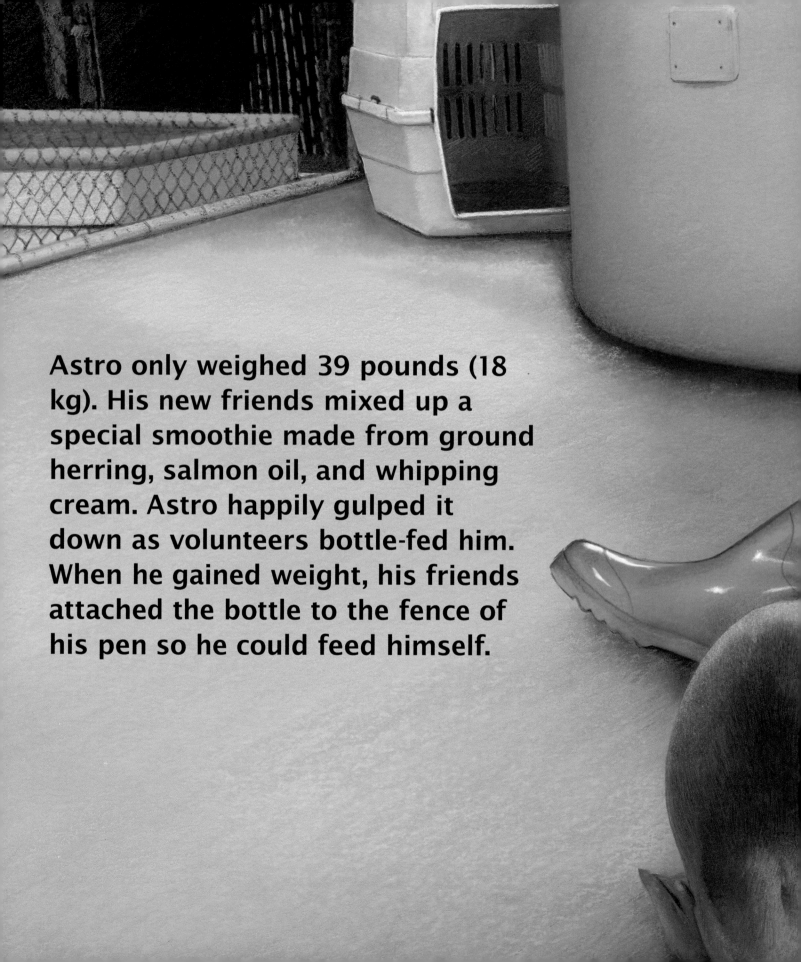

Astro only weighed 39 pounds (18 kg). His new friends mixed up a special smoothie made from ground herring, salmon oil, and whipping cream. Astro happily gulped it down as volunteers bottle-fed him. When he gained weight, his friends attached the bottle to the fence of his pen so he could feed himself.

By the time he was 10 months old, Astro was big enough to join other Steller sea lions in the wild where he belonged. A satellite tag was attached to Astro's back so The Marine Mammal Center would be able to track his travels in the ocean.

His friends took him to the beach where he had been found and set him free in the surf. Astro paddled into the foam. Then a wave hit him. He didn't know what to do. He was scared and scooted out of the water onto the sand.

Astro needed to go into the ocean, not up on the beach with people. Would Astro be able to return to the wild? Was he so young when he was rescued that he attached to people instead of other sea lions?

From far down the beach, Astro's friends watched him. For the next two days, Astro barely went into the water. Instead, he joined the elephant seals on the beach. He was confused. He had not seen the ocean since he was a few days old. The volunteers were worried he would starve.

When Astro didn't leave the beach, his friends decided to take him far out into the ocean, far away from beaches and people. So, they took Astro back to the Center.

The next day, Astro was put on a boat with eight Northern fur seals to be released in the ocean. The nine marine mammals and their friends from the Center traveled to the Farallon Islands, 27 miles west of the Golden Gate Bridge.

As the cages were opened for the eight seals, they each quickly dove into the ocean. Everyone on the boat cheered.

When someone opened Astro's cage, Astro didn't move. His friends waited. Astro still didn't move.

"Go join your pals," urged the boat captain.

Astro didn't budge. His friends tilted the cage. He held on with all four flippers. Finally, he let go. With a huge splash, Astro swam deep into the ocean. His friends cheered.

But . . . 10 days later, Astro swam under the Golden Gate Bridge into the San Francisco Bay. He climbed onto a sandy beach in someone's backyard—not far from The Marine Mammal Center.

Once again, the people from the Center captured Astro and drove him back to his pen. He seemed happy to be back, but his friends were worried. The longer Astro stayed out of the ocean, the harder it would be for him to live in the wild.

After a few days, Astro's friends took him to another island. They hoped he would not return to any beaches with people.

But, Astro had other plans. Just three days later, he swam under the Golden Gate Bridge into the San Francisco Bay. Just like a dog, he had found his way back.

This time he spotted a group of children and their parents on a field next to a school. The people were holding a walk-a-thon to raise money for the school. Astro flopped out of the water and onto the field—he wanted to join in the fun, too! He scooted around the orange cones on the grassy field. He made it all the way around one lap! Everyone cheered for Astro.

But the people also knew Astro needed to return to the ocean. They tried to coax him towards the bay by pretending their buckets were full of food and then swinging the buckets in front of him. Astro didn't leave. He just stayed in the parking lot. The people called The Marine Mammal Center. Once again, the volunteers rescued Astro, and returned him to his pen and saltwater tank.

His friends at The Marine Mammal Center were sad, very sad. They realized that Astro could not live in the ocean. He had been too young when rescued and had attached himself to people instead of Steller sea lions. He would just keep returning to places with people.

He could not stay at The Marine Mammal Center
any longer because it is an animal hospital,
not a place to live. Astro's friends made phone
calls to find him a new home. His friends at the
Center were thrilled when the Mystic Aquarium in
Connecticut said Astro could go there.

Astro's first stop was a six-month stay at the Long
Marine Lab at the University of California in Santa Cruz.

Since Steller sea lions are a threatened species, the
scientists at the lab studied Astro to learn how to
help protect them. They tested Astro's hearing and
looked at how quickly he processed his food.

Astro needed to learn to follow directions. The trainers used a training method called "bridge and target." When Astro learned to touch the trainer's fist (the target) with his nose, the trainer would say "good," (the bridge). Astro connected the "good" with the right behavior. Then the trainer could teach him to follow other directions. Wanting to please the trainers, Astro learned quickly.

Astro was known for his fun personality and liked to greet schoolchildren who visited the Long Marine Lab.

He loved playing with his toys and took them into his kennel when he slept.

Astro flew in an airplane all the way across the United States from California to Connecticut.

Although his friends at The Marine Mammal Center and the Long Marine Laboratory wish that Astro could have returned to the ocean, they are very happy that he has such a wonderful new home. If you're ever in Mystic, Connecticut, be sure to visit him.

For Creative Minds

Steller Sea Lions

The word "stellar" is a descriptive word (adjective) that describes something or someone as being a "star" or a great performer. The word "Steller" with an "e" is a specific species of sea lion (proper noun) named after the naturalist Georg Wilhelm Steller (1700s). So, you could say that Astro is a stellar Steller sea lion!

Rookeries are isolated, rocky coastal areas and islands where sea lions gather to mate and where females give birth to their pups.

Steller sea lions dive deeper than 1,300 feet (400 m) to find food!

Prey: walleye pollack, mackerel, herring, capelin, sand lance, cod, and salmon

Predators: orca whales, humans, and some sharks

Only Native Alaskans who rely on the sea lions are allowed to hunt them. All other hunting is illegal. In addition, commercial fishermen cannot fish within three nautical miles of rookeries.

Adult males can be 11 feet (3.25 m) long and weigh up to 2,500 lb. (1120 kg). Males have long, coarse hair on their necks that looks like a male lion's mane.

The smaller females can be 9 feet (2.9 m) and usually weigh 400 to 600 lb. (181 to 272 kg) but can weigh up to 770 lb. (350 kg).

Steller sea lions' fur is a coarse and light tan to red brown when dry. When wet, it is smooth and slick and lies flat against their skin.

They have a thick layer of fat (blubber) that keeps them warm in cold water.

Steller Sea Lions Threatened and Endangered

There are two main groups of Steller sea lions. The Eastern group lives off the coast of California, up the Pacific Coast to 144° West Longitude in Alaska. This group is threatened, (a species in trouble). The Western group lives west of 144° West Longitude to Japan. That group is endangered (a species in danger of extinction). Scientists are not sure what has caused the Steller sea lions to decrease in numbers. Some possible reasons include:

Commercial fishing competes with the Steller sea lions for fish. Technology has made it much easier for fishermen to find schools of fish, leaving fewer fish for the sea lions.

Pollution kills all kinds of marine animals. It can poison the animals, or sometimes the animals get trapped in garbage (fishing nets or the plastic rings that go around soda cans).

Where in the World? A Map Activity

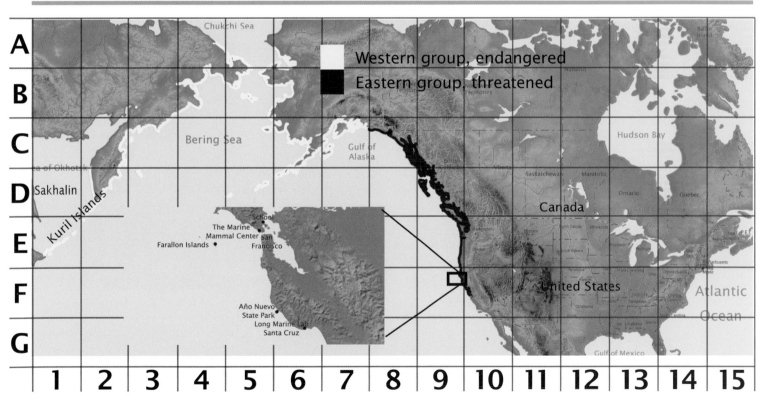

Use the map to find the various locations mentioned below, then put the events in proper chronological (by date) order. Answers are upside-down, below.

1. In April 2007, Astro was taken back to Año Nuevo State Park, but he stayed on the beach. He was then taken to the Farallon Islands.

2. Astro flew in an airplane from California to Mystic, Connecticut in February, 2008.

3. In August 2007, Astro went to the Long Marine Laboratory in Santa Cruz.

4. Astro was found orphaned at Año Nuevo State Park in June 2006.

Date order: 4, 1, 3, 2

Steller Sea Lion Life Cycle

Put the Steller sea lion life-cycle events in order to spell the scrambled word.

A — Pups are born in late May through July. They are about 3.3 feet (1 m) long, weigh 35 to 50 pounds (16-23 kg), and are black or very dark brown in color.

O — Pups molt (shed) their fur when they are about 4 or 5 months, and the new fur is lighter in color. They will then molt several times and by the end of their second year, they will have their adult color.

I — When the pups are 4 to 6 weeks old, they swim for the first time.

E — The females (cows) arrive at the rookery at the end of May or early June and look for good birthing areas. The male may end up with several females to care for. The females, who have been pregnant for a year, give birth to their pup shortly after arriving. They can get pregnant again when their pups are only a few weeks old.

S — In early May, the adult males (bulls) fight for and claim their rookery territory. They generally return to the same area to claim, and it may be several years before they can fight off an older male. Once they "have" their territory, they may hold onto it for a few years until they are too old and weak (13 to 15 years old) to fight off younger males. The fighting for territory consists of roaring, hissing, and chest-to-chest fights with open mouths that sometimes cause severe injury. The winner keeps the best areas and the losers go to smaller, not as nice areas. Males do not leave their territories or eat while waiting for the females to arrive—up to a month.

L — The mother stays with the pups for a week or two before leaving it alone while she goes off to find food. The young pups gather in groups to sleep and play together while their mothers are gone. The mothers and pups find each other by smells and sounds. A cow will not nurse a pup that is not hers. A pup nurses from its mother for at least three months, and will usually nurse until its mother has another pup.

N — Females have their first pups when they are 4 or 5 years old and live about 30 years in the wild. Males, on the other hand, only live to about 18 in the wild, probably because of all the fighting for territory.

Answer: SEA LION

Sea Lion or Seal? What's the Same? What's Different?

Both sea lions and seals are marine mammals, which means they are adapted to life in the ocean and rely on the ocean for their food.

Both get their oxygen from the air.

They are pinnipeds (flipper-footed), an order of marine mammals that also includes walruses. They haul themselves onto land to rest and breed.

They are both carnivores (meat-eating animals).

Steller Sea Lion

Harbor Seal

Sea lions are noisier than seals.

Sea lions have long front flippers and can pull their rear flippers under them so they can "walk" on land. Seals do not "walk"—they slide around on land.

Seals have short front flippers with claws that they use to haul themselves out of the water onto land.

Seals swim with their rear flippers.

Sea lions have external ear flaps, seals do not.

Sea lions swim with their front flippers and use their rear flippers to steer.

Astro is held at the Mystic Aquarium under the authority of NMFS Permit No. 42-1908-00 issued pursuant to the provisions to the Marine Mammal Protection Act and the Endangered Species Act.

The author donates a percentage of her royalties to The Marine Mammal Center and the Mystic Aquarium.

Thanks to Ann Bauer, Director of Education at The Marine Mammal Center, and the staff at Mystic Aquarium, a division of Sea Research Foundation, Inc., for verifying the accuracy of the information in this book.

To my parents, June and Joe Walker, and Kent, my husband, and Will and Scott, my sons, for all their encouragement, and to Astro, a truly stellar Steller sea lion! Special thanks to Jane Oliver (The Marine Mammal Center in Sausalito, CA) and Traci Kendall (the Long Marine Laboratory, UC Santa Cruz), and Astro's current trainer, Erin Sermac (Mystic Aquarium, Mystic, CT) for sharing with me their experiences with Astro — Astro's story is definitely their story, too! And to all the volunteers and staff at The Marine Mammal Center and the Long Marine Lab for their incredible dedication and devotion, and to those at the Mystic Aquarium for their amazing care and warm welcome of Astro.—JWH

While doing research for the illustrations, I traveled from the Mystic Aquarium in CT, to The Marine Mammal Center in Sausalito, CA and the Long Marine Lab in Santa Cruz CA, to the New England Aquarium in Boston, MA. I would especially like to thank Ann Bauer and the staff at The Marine Mammal Center and Traci Kendall and Beau Richter at the Long Marine Lab, UCSC—all for giving up their time and allowing me to tour 'behind the scenes' of their facilities; Matt Pearson of the Marin Country Day School for photos from the Walk-a-thon; the Northern Fur Seals at the New England Aquarium; and Becky Giantonio of the Mystic Aquarium for her help; and, of course, Astro—SB

Publisher's Cataloging-In-Publication Data

Harvey, Jeanne Walker.   Astro : the Steller sea lion/
by Jeanne Walker Harvey ; illustrated by Shennen Bersani.

     p. : col. ill. ; cm.

     Summary: Astro, an orphaned, endangered Steller sea lion, was found and then raised at the Marine Mammal Center in California. When released, he kept swimming back to the Center, just like a lost dog finding his way home. Readers follow Astro through some of his travels that have now taken him across the U.S. to his current home at the Mystic Aquarium in Connecticut. Includes "For Creative Minds" educational section.

ISBN: 978-1-60718-860-5 (hardcover)
ISBN: 978-1-60718-874-2 (paperback)
ISBN: 978-1-60718-101-9 (English downloadable eBook)
ISBN: 978-1-60718-112-5 (Spanish downloadable eBook)
ISBN: 978-1-60718-299-3 (Interactive, read-aloud eBook featuring selectable English and Spanish text and audio (web and iPad/tablet based))
Grade level: P-4
ATOS™ Level: 4.4
Lexile Level: 790 Lexile Code: AD

1. Steller's sea lion--Juvenile non-fiction. 2. Marine animals--Juvenile non-fiction. 3. Steller's sea lion--non-Fiction. 4. Marine animals--non-Fiction. I. Bersani, Shennen. II. Title.

QL706.2 .H37 2010
599.79/75   2010921908

Printed in China, July 2018
This product conforms to CPSIA 2008

Arbordale Publishing
formerly Sylvan Dell Publishing
Mt.. Pleasant, SC 29464
www.ArbordalePublishing.com